www.jbsims.c

MW01204350

"You are here for a reason"

Keep Reading

What are YOU fighting for?

Jeremy B. Sims

Published by Jeremy Sims, 2024.

While every precaution has been taken in the preparation of this book, the publisher assumes no responsibility for errors or omissions, or for damages resulting from the use of the information contained herein.

WHAT ARE YOU FIGHTING FOR?

First edition. February 4, 2024.

Copyright © 2024 Jeremy B. Sims.

ISBN: 979-8224127627

Written by Jeremy B. Sims.

Also by Jeremy B. Sims

GOT HUMILITY?

Watch for more at https://www.jbsims.com/.

Table of Contents

Preface

I *ntroduction to the Book's Purpose and Inspiration*

In a world where battles are often perceived through the lens of physical conflicts and material pursuits, "What Are You Fighting For?" seeks to delve deeper into the essence of our struggles. This book draws inspiration from the spiritual wisdom of the ages, particularly the profound message found in Ephesians 6:12 of the King James Bible, which reminds us that our true battles are not against flesh and blood but against much greater forces. This biblical foundation sets the stage for an exploration into the myriad of challenges we face in modern society—challenges that test our character, beliefs, and values.

The purpose of this book is not only to illuminate the unseen battles we fight but also to guide you toward identifying what is truly worth fighting for. Through examining the juxtaposition of spiritual warfare against cultural, societal, and personal battles, this book aims to offer a beacon of light for those navigating the complexities of life. It is an invitation to reflect on our personal journeys, the societal norms we contend with, and the cultural biases that shape our perspectives.

―――――――

BRIEF EXPLORATION OF the Biblical Quote from Ephesians 6:12

Ephesians 6:12 serves as a cornerstone for our discussion: "For we wrestle not against flesh and blood, but against principalities, against powers, against the rulers of the darkness of this world, against spiritual wickedness in high places." This passage is a powerful reminder that our true adversaries are not the people or the systems we see before us but the underlying forces of negativity, injustice, and spiritual decay that pervade our world.

This preface aims to unpack this concept, setting a foundation for the themes discussed throughout the book. It is a call to readers to look beyond the surface, to understand the deeper significance of their struggles, and to choose their battles wisely. In doing so, we embark on a journey toward personal greatness, armed with honesty, truth, and a heart free of envy and jealousy. We learn to cherish positive change, embrace a willingness to learn from our mistakes, and cultivate persistence, patience, true love, and goodwill.

As we turn the pages, let us embark on this journey together, exploring the battles worth fighting for, armed with the knowledge that our greatest victories lie not in conquering external adversaries but in overcoming the challenges within ourselves and our societies. This is not just a book; it is a journey towards understanding, a manual for personal growth, and a call to action for all who seek a life of meaning and purpose.

Chapter 1: The Battle Beyond the Physical

———

As we step into the heart of our journey with "*What Are You Fighting For?*", we embark on a profound exploration of spiritual warfare—a concept deeply rooted in biblical teachings yet universally relevant across cultures and beliefs. This chapter is not merely an academic discussion; it is an invitation to understand and engage with the invisible battles that shape our existence and our world.

Spiritual Warfare: A Biblical Perspective

The Bible presents spiritual warfare as an unseen conflict raging in the spiritual realm, a battle between the forces of good and evil that influences our lives and our world in ways we may not always perceive. Ephesians 6:12, as introduced in the preface, offers a clear depiction of this struggle, emphasizing that our real enemies are not of flesh and blood. This concept extends beyond mere religious doctrine; it is a universal truth about the nature of the struggles we face—struggles against **greed, hatred, injustice, and despair just to name a few.**

Beyond Religion: A Universal Struggle

However, the essence of spiritual warfare transcends the confines of any single religion or belief system. It is a metaphor for the internal and societal conflicts we all experience, regardless of our cultural background or faith. Every culture, every religion, and every philosophical tradition has its own way of understanding and articulating this battle between light and darkness, between virtue and vice.

In recognizing this, we open ourselves to a more inclusive and persuasive understanding of spiritual warfare. It's not just about the Christian perspective; it's about acknowledging that, across the world, individuals are fighting their own versions of this battle, armed with the teachings and traditions of their own cultures and religions. This shared struggle offers a common ground for dialogue, understanding, and mutual respect.

Engaging with Diverse Perspectives

This chapter encourages you to approach spiritual warfare with an open mind and heart. By exploring how different cultures and religions perceive the struggle between good and evil, we can enrich our own understanding and find commonalities that unite us in our human experience. Such an exploration is not about diluting our beliefs but about deepening them through the wisdom of others.

We invite you to consider spiritual warfare not just as a religious concept but as a universal experience—a lens through which we can view our personal battles and societal challenges. This perspective empowers us to fight against not only personal failings like envy, jealousy, and dishonesty but also against societal and cultural biases, perspectives, and opinions that sow division and discord.

A Call to Open Dialogue and Personal Exploration

Let this be a call to open dialogue and personal exploration. Engage with the teachings of your own tradition, but also be willing to listen and learn from the experiences and beliefs of others. Whether through the lens of Christianity, Buddhism, Islam, Hinduism, secular humanism, or any other worldviews, we can find valuable insights and common ground.

As we navigate the complexities of spiritual warfare, let us do so with humility, respect, and a genuine willingness to understand. This is not a journey of conversion but of conversation—a conversation that enriches our spiritual lives and guides us toward personal growth, unity, and a deeper understanding of the battles we all face.

———————

THIS CHAPTER LAYS THE foundation for a journey of exploration, not just within the pages of sacred texts but within the depths of our own hearts and minds. It is an invitation to explore what works best for your personal journey, free from bias, perspective, or opinion. **May we all find the courage to face our battles with wisdom, strength, and an open heart, building bridges of understanding that span the vast and rich diversity of human belief and experience.**

In this journey, we delve into a concept that, while originating in spiritual texts, transcends religious boundaries and speaks to the core of the human experience. It's about recognizing that the essence of our struggles—our battles against internal weaknesses and societal injustices—is shared across all creeds and cultures. This chapter is an invitation to simplify and universalize this exploration, making it accessible and relevant to everyone, including those who do not adhere to any religion.

Understanding Our Common Ground

Regardless of religious belief or the lack thereof, each person experiences internal conflicts and external challenges that test their character, values, and principles. These battles are not reserved for the religious; they are the essence of the human condition. An atheist, a theist, and an agnostic all face moral dilemmas, ethical choices, and the pursuit of meaning in their lives. This commonality is our starting point for a journey of exploration.

The Battle Within

At its core, spiritual warfare—or, more broadly, the battle between good and evil—can be understood as the struggle to overcome our lesser instincts and strive for a higher standard of thought, action, and existence. For some, this is a quest to align with divine will; for others, it is a pursuit of the best version of oneself or the contribution to a more just and compassionate world.

For the Believer: *This might mean seeking alignment with divine principles, striving for virtues extolled in sacred texts, and combating the vices that those texts warn against.*

For the Atheist or Agnostic: *The battle might be framed in terms of personal integrity, ethical living, and the pursuit of truth and justice, without reference to a higher power but with a commitment to the values that ensure a harmonious and equitable society.*

The Battle Against Societal and Cultural Biases

This battle extends beyond personal transformation to the collective effort of challenging and overcoming societal and cultural biases, perspectives, and opinions that hinder progress and foster division. Recognizing these external battles requires critical thinking, empathy, and the willingness to engage in difficult conversations.

Engagement Without Bias: *Approach discussions with openness, seeking to understand different viewpoints without the need to convert or convince. This fosters a culture of learning and mutual respect.*

Exploration of Values: *Examine the values that underpin different cultures and religions, identifying universal principles such as justice, compassion, and integrity that can unite us in our shared humanity.*

A Journey of Personal Exploration

This journey is deeply personal and uniquely tailored to everyone's experiences, beliefs, and aspirations. It's about asking fundamental questions: *What kind of person do I want to be?*

What values do I want to live by?

How can I contribute to making the world a better place?

For the Religious: *This might involve a deeper dive into one's faith, understanding how spiritual teachings can inform and guide one's actions and decisions.*

For the Non-Religious: *It involves a similar quest for meaning and purpose, grounded in a secular but no less profound commitment to ethical principles and personal growth.*

An Invitation to All

This chapter extends an invitation to all—believers, non-believers, and those in between—to engage in a process of self-examination and world exploration free from preconceived notions. It's an encouragement to step beyond the confines of dogma and doctrine, into a space where we can freely explore what it means to live a good life, make ethical choices, and contribute to a world characterized by understanding, respect, and compassion.

Through this inclusive and open-ended approach, we can all embark on a journey of discovery that respects our differences while celebrating our shared quest for meaning, purpose, and a better world. This is not just a chapter in a book; it's a chapter in each of our lives, inviting us to explore, question, and grow in ways that resonate with our personal journey.

Chapter 2: The Enemies We Face - A Universal Perspective

———

In "The Enemies We Face," we dive into understanding the adversaries that challenge us, both seen and unseen. These enemies, described in spiritual texts as principalities, powers, rulers of darkness, and spiritual wickedness, serve as metaphors for the broader, more universal struggles that all humans confront, regardless of their cultural, religious, or philosophical backgrounds. This chapter aims to bridge the gap between these ancient concepts and the modern-day battles we face, offering a persuasive guide for learners from all walks of life to explore these ideas in a manner that resonates with their personal journey.

Unpacking the Metaphors

The *"enemies"* mentioned in sacred texts symbolize the forces that work against our highest good and societal harmony. Let's break these down into more relatable terms:

Principalities and Powers: These can be likened to the systemic structures and institutions that perpetuate injustice, inequality, and oppression. In today's context, this might refer to systemic racism, gender inequality, economic disparities, and other forms of institutionalized discrimination.

Rulers of Darkness: This metaphor can represent the spread of misinformation, ignorance, and the deliberate obscuration of truth that plagues our information age. It's the darkness of falsehood that clouds judgment and stirs conflict.

Spiritual Wickedness in High Places: Often, this can be interpreted as the corrupting influence of power and the moral compromises made by those in positions of authority. It speaks to ethical decay and the loss of integrity among leaders, which can lead to widespread societal harm.

Modern Analogies for a Universal Battle

Each of these metaphors has a counterpart in the challenges we face in our personal lives and as a global community. By understanding these analogies, we can start to identify the "enemies" in our midst:

Systemic Injustice: The structures and norms that perpetuate inequality and hinder progress towards a more equitable society.

Misinformation: The rampant spread of false information that fuels division, fear, and misunderstanding.

Internal Struggles: The personal battles we face with our own shortcomings, such as greed, envy, and hatred, which mirror the external challenges of societal wickedness.

A Journey of Exploration for All

This exploration is not confined to those who adhere to religious beliefs; it extends to atheists, agnostics, and individuals from all cultural backgrounds. It is an invitation to reflect on the universal "enemies" we face and to discover the tools and strategies that work best for our personal growth and societal contribution.

For the Religious: This journey might involve drawing on the wisdom of spiritual traditions to confront and overcome these challenges, seeking guidance from sacred texts and religious teachings.

For the Non-Religious: The focus may be on ethical principles, critical thinking, and the development of personal virtues as means to combat the forces of injustice, misinformation, and moral decay.

Engaging in Open Dialogue

This chapter encourages an open dialogue, inviting readers to share their experiences and insights on facing these "enemies." By engaging in conversation without bias, we can learn from each other, regardless of our background, and find common ground in our shared human experience.

———

A CALL TO ACTION

"The Enemies We Face" concludes with a call to action, urging readers to identify the forces that challenge them personally and societally. It encourages a commitment to personal development and societal engagement, advocating for a proactive stance against the injustices and struggles that hinder our collective progress.

This chapter is not just about recognizing the enemies; it's about mobilizing our collective wisdom, strength, and compassion to confront them. It invites each of us to embark on a journey of exploration, self-reflection, and action, free from bias, and open to discovering what truly resonates with our personal path towards growth and societal contribution.

Self-Assessment: Mobilizing Personal Perspectives and Journeys

As we conclude the chapter on "The Enemies We Face," the call to action not only seeks to recognize and confront the universal challenges but also emphasizes the importance of self-assessment in mobilizing our personal perspectives and journeys. This section is dedicated to guiding readers through a self-assessment process that honors all universal perspectives, encouraging individuals to reflect deeply on their personal battles, strengths, weaknesses, and their unique path forward.

Step 1: Identifying Your Battles

Reflect on the "Enemies": Consider the metaphors of principalities, powers, rulers of darkness, and spiritual wickedness.

How do these manifests in your life, both externally and internally?

Are there systemic injustices you are passionate about?

Misinformation you want tocorrect?

Personal vices you need to overcome?

———————————

UNIVERSAL PERSPECTIVE: Acknowledge that these battles are not unique to any one culture or belief system but are part of the human experience.

How does recognizing the universality of these challenges affect your perspective on them?

Step 2: Assessing Your Strengths and Weaknesses

Personal Inventory: Take stock of your strengths—those qualities that equip you to fight your battles. These might include resilience, empathy, critical thinking, or spiritual faith. Conversely, acknowledge your weaknesses or areas for growth, such as susceptibility to misinformation, indifference to systemic injustices, or personal vices.

Growth Mindset: From a universal perspective, consider how different cultures or belief systems view personal growth and transformation. How can these views inform or enrich your understanding of your own strengths and weaknesses?

Step 3: Mobilizing Your Personal Journey

Action Plan: Based on your assessment, create a personal action plan. This could involve educating yourself on issues of injustice, engaging in community service, developing a personal meditation or prayer practice, or seeking dialogues that challenge and expand your worldview.

Universal Engagement: Reflect on how your actions, informed by your personal and cultural perspectives, contribute to a larger, universal fight against the "enemies" we face. How does your journey intersect with those of others from different backgrounds or belief systems?

Step 4: Commitment to Open Dialogue

Sharing and Listening: Commit to sharing your journey and learning from others. Open dialogue can be a powerful tool for personal and communal growth.

How can you engage in conversations that bridge differences and foster mutual understanding?

Universal Solidarity: Consider how your commitment to open dialogue and learning from diverse perspectives can mobilize others.

How does fostering understanding across differences contribute to the universal battle against the enemies we face?

A Personal and Collective Call to Action

This self-assessment is not just an exercise in personal reflection; it's a call to action that recognizes the power of individual journeys in contributing to a collective effort. By taking stock of our personal battles, strengths, and weaknesses, and by mobilizing our unique perspectives and experiences, we not only advance our own growth but also contribute to the larger, universal fight against injustice, misinformation, and moral decay.

This is a reminder that each personal journey, informed by a diverse array of cultural and philosophical perspectives, enriches the tapestry of our collective human experience. As we mobilize personal perspectives and embark on our individual journeys, we do so not in isolation but as part of a broader, interconnected effort to create a world characterized by understanding, compassion, and justice for all.

Chapter 3: Foundations Worth Fighting For

———

In the heart of our quest to understand *"What Are You Fighting For?"* lies the exploration of the core virtues that not only define our personal journey but also have the power to transform societies. This chapter delves into the essence of personal greatness, honesty, truth, and a mind free of envy and jealousy. We aim to persuade and guide learners from all backgrounds, cultures, and belief systems to see these virtues not just as ideals but as practical, foundational elements that can significantly enhance one's life and the world at large.

Personal Greatness: The Pursuit of Excellence

Universal Appeal: Personal greatness transcends cultural and religious boundaries, embodying the pursuit of one's highest potential. It's about striving for excellence in all areas of life—personal, professional, and spiritual. This virtue is recognized and celebrated in countless philosophies and faiths across the globe, each offering unique insights into the journey toward achieving it.

Empowering Individuals and Societies: Personal greatness inspires others and can lead to positive societal change. When individuals commit to bettering themselves, they set a powerful example for others, creating a ripple effect that can transform communities and, ultimately, societies.

Honesty: The Foundation of Trust

Cross-Cultural Virtue: Honesty is valued universally, serving as the bedrock of trust and integrity in relationships, communities, and entire societies. It encourages transparency and fosters trust, two elements critical for the healthy functioning of any group or society.

Building Societal Cohesion: Honesty in governance, business, and personal relationships builds a culture of trust, which is essential for social cohesion and cooperation. When people believe in the honesty of their leaders and each other, it creates a more stable and harmonious society.

Truth: Seeking Clarity in a Complex World

A Universal Quest: The pursuit of truth is a fundamental human endeavor that cuts across all divides. Every culture and religion hold the concept of truth in high regard, albeit with different interpretations. Engaging in open dialogue about these varied perspectives can enrich our understanding and appreciation of truth.

Empowerment through Knowledge: Understanding and acknowledging truth empowers individuals and societies to make informed decisions. It combats ignorance and misinformation, paving the way for enlightenment and progress.

A Mind Free of Envy and Jealousy: Cultivating Contentment and Compassion

Common Human Challenge: Envy and jealousy are emotions experienced universally, yet many traditions teach the importance of overcoming these feelings. By examining how various cultures and religions address these emotions, we can find practical strategies for cultivating contentment and compassion.

Enhancing Social Harmony: A society where individuals are content with themselves and compassionate towards others is more likely to be peaceful and cooperative. Overcoming envy and jealousy not only benefits personal well-being but also contributes to a more supportive and less competitive community.

Inviting Open Dialogue and Exploration

This chapter is an open invitation to explore these virtues through the lens of your own culture, religion, or philosophical beliefs. Engaging in this exploration can reveal how these foundational elements are valued and implemented across different traditions, offering insights that might resonate with your personal journey.

Reflect on Personal and Cultural Understandings: Take time to reflect on how these virtues are understood and practiced in your own life and within your cultural or religious context. *What lessons can you learn from other traditions that might enhance your personal development or societal contribution?*

Engage in Inter-Cultural Dialogue: Share your insights and learn from others. This exchange can deepen your appreciation of these universal virtues and inspire innovative ways to incorporate them into your life and community.

A Call to Personal and Societal Transformation

"Foundations Worth Fighting For" concludes with a persuasive call to action, urging readers to embrace and cultivate these virtues in their lives. By doing so, individuals not only embark on a path of personal fulfillment and greatness but also contribute to building stronger, more honest, and compassionate societies. This chapter challenges us to break down the barriers of bias, perspective, and opinion, and to engage in a shared journey of exploration and growth that honors the diversity of human experience and the universal quest for a better world.

Creating an environment that fosters personal greatness, honesty, truth, and a mindset free of envy and jealousy requires intentional actions across various aspects of our lives. Implementing a self-assessment that focuses on cultivating these virtues in oneself, at home, within social circles, in educational settings, and in religious or organizational contexts is a holistic approach to nurturing a positive and transformative environment. Here's a guide to embarking on this journey:

Personal Self-Assessment

Identify Your Values: Reflect on the importance of personal greatness, honesty, truth, and being free from envy and jealousy.

How do these values manifest in your daily life?

Set Personal Goals: Based on your reflection, set specific, achievable goals to strengthen these virtues within yourself. This could include daily affirmations, mindfulness practices, or setting aside time for self-reflection.

At Home

Model Virtues: Demonstrate these values through your actions. Be honest and open in your communication with family members, and show appreciation for their qualities and achievements without envy.

Create Open Dialogue: Encourage family discussions about the importance of these virtues. Share stories or examples from various cultures or religions that highlight their value.

In Social Environments

Lead by Example: In your circle of friends and broader social network, be a role model for honesty, truthfulness, and celebrating others' successes without envy.

Promote Positive Conversations: Steer discussions toward positive topics that encourage sharing successes and challenges openly, without fear of judgment or envy.

In Schools of All Ages

Integrate Virtues into the Curriculum: Advocate for the inclusion of lessons on personal development and ethics that emphasize these core virtues. This could be through literature, history, or social studies classes.

Encourage Virtue-Based Projects: Support projects and group work that focus on collaboration and mutual respect. Highlight the importance of honesty and truth in academic work.

IN CHURCHES AND ORGANIZATIONS

Incorporate Virtues into Teachings: In religious settings, integrate discussions of these virtues into sermons, study groups, or youth programs, drawing on scriptural or philosophical texts that emphasize their importance.

Foster a Supportive Community: Create programs or groups within organizations that focus on personal growth, ethical leadership, and community service, encouraging honesty, truth, and supportiveness.

Action Steps for Implementation

Reflect and Journal: Regularly assess your progress in fostering these environments. Journaling can help track changes and growth over time.

Seek Feedback: Ask for feedback from family, friends, colleagues, or community members on how your efforts are impacting the environment around you.

Adjust and Adapt: Be prepared to adjust your strategies based on feedback and the evolving needs of your community.

Share and Inspire: Share your journey and the lessons learned with others. Your story can inspire others to embark on a similar path of fostering an environment rooted in these fundamental virtues.

By taking these steps, you can contribute to creating a more honest, compassionate, and supportive environment across all areas of your life. This self-assessment and action plan is not a one-time effort but a continuous journey of growth, learning, and positive influence.

Chapter 4: The Tools for the Fight

———

I n the journey towards personal and societal transformation, knowing what we are fighting for is just the beginning. Equally important is equipping ourselves with the right tools for the fight. This chapter delves into the strategies and virtues necessary for cultivating positive change, learning from our mistakes, and nurturing persistence, patience, true love, and goodwill. We aim to provide a persuasive and inclusive guide that resonates with learners from all walks of life, encouraging exploration and application of these tools within various cultural and religious contexts.

Cultivating Positive Change

Actionable Steps: Begin with small, achievable goals that lead to positive change. Volunteer, engage in community service, or simply commit to acts of kindness in your daily life. These actions, though small, create ripples that can inspire larger societal shifts.

Universal Principles: Recognize that the desire for a better world transcends cultural and religious boundaries. Engage in intercultural dialogue to learn how different communities enact positive change and incorporate these lessons into your own efforts.

———

LEARNING FROM MISTAKES

Embracing Failure as a Teacher: View mistakes not as setbacks but as opportunities for growth. Cultivate a mindset that welcomes constructive criticism and is open to learning from every experience.

Cross-Cultural Wisdom: Explore teachings from various cultures and religions that emphasize the value of learning from failure. This can provide a broader perspective and reinforce the universality of growth through adversity.

Persistence and Patience

Developing Resilience: Persistence is about staying the course despite obstacles, while patience involves waiting for the right moment to act. Develop resilience by setting long-term goals and breaking them down into manageable steps.

Inspirational Stories: Draw inspiration from historical figures, spiritual leaders, and everyday heroes from across the world who exemplify persistence and patience. Their stories can motivate us to keep moving forward, even when progress seems slow.

———

TRUE LOVE AND GOODWILL

Cultivating Compassion: True love and goodwill towards others start with empathy and understanding. Practice active listening and strive to see situations from others' perspectives.

Global Traditions of Love and Goodwill: Learn from the diverse ways in which love and goodwill are expressed and nurtured in different cultures and religions. This can enrich your own practice of these virtues.

Importance of Personal Development and Self-Reflection

Commitment to Growth: Personal development is a lifelong journey. Dedicate time regularly for self-reflection, meditation, or prayer, whatever aligns with your beliefs, to contemplate your progress and areas for improvement.

Learning from the Global Community: Engage with philosophies, spiritual practices, and personal development techniques from around the world. This open-minded approach can provide new tools and insights for your journey.

Engaging in Open Dialogue and Exploration

This chapter is not just a list of strategies but an invitation to engage with these concepts deeply and personally. It encourages readers to:

Reflect on Their Own Practices: How do you currently employ these tools in your life?

Are there practices from other cultures or belief systems that might enhance your approach?

Participate in Community Learning: Share your experiences and learn from others in your community. This exchange can be a rich source of inspiration and encouragement.

A Personal Toolkit for Transformation

As we conclude this chapter, remember that the journey is as unique as the individual. The tools discussed here are universal, yet how we apply them is deeply personal. This exploration across cultures and beliefs not only broadens our perspective but also deepens our understanding of the common humanity we share. Armed with these tools, we are better equipped to fight for what truly matters, fostering an environment of growth, love, and positive change within ourselves and our communities.

A SELF-ASSESSMENT TOOLKIT

This toolkit accommodates diverse perspectives and needs—including those of religious and non-religious individuals, introverts and extroverts, as well as people with disabilities or who are neurodivergent—requires a thoughtful approach that respects and integrates the uniqueness of each individual's journey. This toolkit aims to provide flexible strategies and reflective questions that can be adapted to fit various life experiences and personal preferences.

For Religious and Non-Religious People

Values Reflection: Identify core values that guide your life.

How do these align with or differ from the teachings of your faith or personal philosophy?

Inspirational Sources: What are your sources of inspiration and guidance?

For religious individuals, this might include sacred texts or spiritual leaders.

For non-religious individuals, this might involve philosophy, science, or personal role models.

COMMUNITY ENGAGEMENT: How do you engage with your community in ways that reflect your beliefs or values?

Consider both religious communities and secular groups or organizations.

For Introverts and Extroverts

Social Interaction: Reflect on your preferred styles of social interaction and how they influence your ability to enact positive change or engage with your community.

How can you leverage your natural tendencies (whether introverted or extroverted) to support your goals?

Energy Management: Consider how social interactions affect your energy levels.

What strategies can you use to recharge and maintain your well-being while pursuing your objectives?

Communication Styles: How do your communication preferences align with your approach to personal development and activism?

Identify ways to adapt your style to different contexts and audiences.

FOR PEOPLE WITH DISABILITIES or Who Are Neurodivergent

Accessibility and Inclusion: Assess the accessibility and inclusivity of your environment.

How can you advocate for changes that support your needs and the needs of others?

Strengths-Based Approach: Identify your unique strengths and how they can be applied to your personal development goals and contributions to society.

Consider how your experiences provide unique insights into challenges and solutions.

Support Systems: Evaluate your support systems and networks. How can you strengthen these networks to support your journey?

Consider both formal supports (like therapy or accommodations) and informal supports (like friends or online communities).

Toolkit Components

Reflective Journaling: Maintain a journal to regularly reflect on your experiences, challenges, and progress related to the areas outlined above.

GOAL SETTING: Use SMART (Specific, Measurable, Achievable, Relevant, Time-bound) goals to outline clear steps for personal development and community engagement, tailored to your unique situation.

Resource List: Compile a list of resources, including books, websites, and community organizations, that align with your interests and needs. This should be diverse to cover a range of perspectives and support systems.

Self-Care Plan: Develop a self-care plan that respects your personal energy levels, needs, and preferences. This plan should include activities for mental, emotional, and physical well-being.

Mentorship or Peer Support: Seek out mentorship or peer support groups that resonate with your identity and goals. This can provide valuable guidance, encouragement, and a sense of community.

Feedback Mechanism: Establish a method for receiving constructive feedback on your goals and progress. This could be through trusted friends, family, mentors, or support groups.

THIS SELF-ASSESSMENT toolkit is designed to be adaptable, recognizing the diverse ways in which individuals engage with their personal development and societal contributions. By reflecting on and utilizing these tools, individuals from any background, personality type, or ability level can find meaningful ways to grow and make a difference in their communities. The key is to approach this journey with openness, flexibility, and a commitment to inclusivity, allowing for a rich exploration of what works best for your personal journey.

Chapter 5: Misguided Battles

———

In our journey to discern "What Are You Fighting For?", it becomes crucial to recognize not just the battles worth waging but also those that can lead us astray. This chapter delves into societal obsessions and personal pitfalls that, while seemingly important on the surface, often divert us from our true paths. Through a persuasive analysis, we invite learners from all backgrounds, cultures, and belief systems to critically evaluate these misguided battles and to explore more fulfilling alternatives that align with their personal journeys.

Societal Obsessions: Status, Celebrity Culture, and Unachievable Dreams

The Illusion of Status: Society often measures success by material wealth, job titles, or social media followers, pushing us into a relentless pursuit of status. Yet, this quest can leave us feeling empty, as true fulfillment comes from living in alignment with our values and contributing to our communities. Reflect on what success means to you, beyond societal benchmarks.

Celebrity Culture Drawbacks: While admiring celebrities can be harmless, obsession with celebrity culture can skew our understanding of success and happiness. It's important to recognize the curated nature of public personas and focus on cultivating our own talents and virtues.

How can you appreciate art and achievement without losing sight of your own worth and journey?

Chasing Unachievable Dreams: Ambition is valuable, but when dreams are not grounded in reality or aligned with our true selves, they can lead to disappointment. By setting realistic goals and celebrating small victories, we can find joy in the journey towards our dreams. Consider adjusting your aspirations to reflect your personal values and capabilities.

The Pitfalls of Overreliance on Opinions, Therapy Without Action, and Hollow Hypotheses

Opinions vs. Truth: While seeking advice is part of learning and growth, overreliance on others' opinions can cloud our judgment and hinder our self-trust. Cultivate the ability to listen to others while also honing your intuition and critical thinking skills.

How can you balance external advice with internal wisdom?

Therapy Without Action: Therapy and counseling can be powerful tools for personal development, but they are most effective when paired with action. Reflect on the insights gained from therapy or self-help resources and implement changes in your life.

What steps can you take today to apply what you've learned?

Questioning Hollow Hypotheses: Society and culture often present us with hypotheses about what will make us happy or successful. It's crucial to question these narratives and test them against our experiences and values. Engage in a process of exploration and experimentation to discover what truly brings you fulfillment.

Inviting Open Dialogue and Exploration

This chapter encourages an open, reflective dialogue about the societal pressures and personal habits that may be leading us away from our true purposes. By engaging with diverse perspectives and questioning the status quo, we can pave the way for a more authentic and meaningful existence.

Reflect on Personal and Cultural Influences: Examine how your cultural background and personal experiences have shaped your views on success, happiness, and fulfillment. How can you redefine these concepts to better suit your journey?

Engage in Community Discussions: Share your reflections with others and listen to their experiences. This exchange can offer valuable insights and foster a supportive environment for questioning and growth.

Choosing Your Battles Wisely

"Misguided Battles" challenges us to examine the paths we're on critically and to discern whether they lead to true fulfillment. By identifying and stepping away from societal obsessions and personal pitfalls, we open ourselves to a journey of genuine growth, grounded in our values and enriched by our diverse experiences. This chapter is a call to action to engage in battles worth fighting—those that lead to personal development, meaningful connections, and a positive impact on the world.

PAUSEBREAK

A True SELF ASSESSMENT ON NEXT PAGES TO FOLLOW

PAUSE BREAK and DO the WORK

Turning away from societal benchmarks of success to focusing on personal values, beliefs, and achievable goals is a commendable journey towards self-fulfillment and authenticity. While the allure of glitter and glamour can be tempting, finding true contentment often lies in simpler, more personal achievements. Here's a guide to help you navigate this path amid the distractions of societal "gold":

Step 1: Define Your Own Success

Personal Reflection: Dedicate time to reflect on what makes you genuinely happy and fulfilled. This might include career achievements, relationships, personal growth, or hobbies. Remember, success is deeply personal and varies from one individual to another.

Journaling: Start a journal to document your thoughts, feelings, and daily achievements. This practice can help you identify patterns and clarify what aspects of life truly contribute to your sense of success.

Step 2: Align With Your Values

Identify Your Core Values: Make a list of your core values. These could include integrity, compassion, creativity, or family. Understanding what you value most will guide your decisions and actions, leading to a more fulfilling life.

Value-Based Decision Making: Before making decisions, ask yourself whether the outcome aligns with your values. This can help you avoid being swayed by external pressures and focus on what truly matters to you.

Step 3: Set Achievable Goals

SMART Goals: Use the SMART framework (Specific, Measurable, Achievable, Relevant, Time-bound) to set goals. Ensure your goals align with your personal definition of success and your core values.

Celebrate Small Wins: Acknowledge and celebrate your achievements, no matter how small. This reinforces a positive relationship with yourself and keeps you motivated.

Step 4: Reduce Exposure to Societal "Gold"

Curate Your Media Consumption: Be selective about the media you consume. Limit exposure to content that glorifies materialism or unrealistic standards of success.

Mindful Social Media Use: Social media can amplify feelings of inadequacy. Try to follow accounts that inspire and uplift you, rather than those that fuel comparison and discontent.

Step 5: Cultivate Contentment

Gratitude Practice: Regularly practicing gratitude can shift your focus from what you lack to what you have. Consider keeping a gratitude journal or sharing what you're grateful for with loved ones.

Mindfulness and Meditation: These practices can help you stay present and appreciate the current moment, reducing the desire for external validation.

Step 6: Seek Supportive Communities

Find Like-Minded Individuals: Surround yourself with people who share your values and support your definition of success. This could be through clubs, online communities, or informal gatherings.

Mentorship and Guidance: Seek mentors who embody your ideal balance of success and contentment. Their guidance can be invaluable in navigating your own path.

Step 7: Continuous Self-Reflection

Regular Check-ins: Periodically review your goals, values, and definition of success. Life changes, and so may your conception of what it means to be successful.

Adjust and Adapt: Be open to adjusting your goals and values as you grow and learn. Flexibility is key to maintaining alignment with your evolving self.

Shifting focus from societal gold to personal fulfillment is a deeply personal journey that requires introspection, commitment, and resilience. By defining your own success, aligning with your values, setting achievable goals, and cultivating a positive relationship with yourself, you can build a life that feels rich and rewarding on your own terms. Remember, the truest gold lies within the contentment and peace you find in living authentically.

IF YOU HAVE successfully completed the previous pages homework you may continue on but if not attempt to get success on doing the actual work before chapter six starts!!!

Chapter 6: The Personal Journey

―――――

Congratulations you made it so let's start with your personal journey and further this content by building our own personal relationship.

In the quest for what truly matters, "The Personal Journey" stands as a pivotal chapter, underscoring the essence of traversing a path uniquely one's own. This journey is not measured by the milestones of societal achievements but by the steps taken towards discovering personal peace and joy. It's a narrative that champions the individual's quest for fulfillment, advocating for a life lived in harmony with one's deepest values and aspirations, unfettered by the clamor of external opinions and societal pressures.

Embracing the Individual Journey

Unique Paths to Fulfillment: Acknowledge that each person's route to happiness and contentment is as unique as their fingerprint. What brings joy to one may not resonate with another. It's essential to honor your personal inclinations and passions, even when they diverge from the mainstream or the expected.

Inner Peace as a Compass: Let inner peace and joy be your compass, guiding your decisions and actions. This might mean prioritizing activities that nourish your soul, relationships that uplift you, and goals that truly resonate with your inner self.

NAVIGATING EXTERNAL Influences

Resisting Societal Pressures: Society often prescribes a formula for success and happiness, laden with material achievements, status, and perpetual busyness.

Challenge these narratives by asking yourself what genuinely enriches your life.

Cultivate the courage to pursue a path that aligns with your personal values, even if it deviates from societal expectations.

Critical Engagement with Opinions: While feedback from others can be valuable, it's crucial to discern which advice serves your growth and which detracts from your authenticity.

Develop the skill to listen to others without losing your own voice in the process.

Tools for the Journey

Self-Reflection and Mindfulness: Regular self-reflection and mindfulness practices can deepen your understanding of what brings you peace and joy. They enable you to live more consciously and make choices that align with your true self.

Journaling: Keeping a journal can be a powerful tool for tracking your journey, reflecting on your growth, and clarifying your aspirations. It serves as a tangible reminder of your progress and a space for dialogue with yourself.

Building Supportive Networks: Surround yourself with individuals who respect your journey and support your quest for personal fulfillment. A community that nurtures your individuality can be instrumental in helping you maintain your path amidst external pressures.

Embracing Change and Growth

Openness to Evolution: Recognize that your journey is not static. Your understanding of peace and joy may evolve as you encounter new experiences and insights. Embrace this evolution as a natural part of your personal growth.

Resilience in the Face of Challenges: Understand that the journey will have its challenges and setbacks. These moments are not detours but integral parts of the journey, offering lessons and opportunities for growth.

Your Journey, Your Terms

"The Personal Journey" chapter is a celebration of the individual's quest for authenticity and fulfillment. It's an encouragement to carve out a path that resonates with your deepest self, free from the weight of external expectations. This journey is about discovering and nurturing your peace and joy, on your terms. As you turn each page of your life, remember that the most profound achievements are those that bring you closer to your true self, fostering a life of contentment, purpose, and happiness.

Chapter 7: Building a Harmonious Society

———

In a world teeming with diversity, the quest for a harmonious society—one that celebrates differences, understands individual battles, and fosters a deep sense of community—is more critical than ever. This chapter lays out a compelling vision and actionable strategies to construct the foundations of such a society. It is a call to action, a reminder that our strength lies in our diversity and that empathy and unity are not just ideals but necessities for our collective well-being.

A Vision for Unity in Diversity

Imagine a society where every individual, regardless of their background, abilities, challenges, or beliefs, is recognized and valued not just despite their differences but because of them. In this society, the battles of each person—whether they stem from disability, disease, racial or gender identity, class struggles, or the journey between faith and secularism—are not fought in isolation but are understood and supported by the community at large.

Strategies for Communal Support and Understanding

Empathy Education: Integrate empathy training into educational curricula across all levels, from early childhood to university and adult learning programs. Teach empathy not as an abstract concept but as a practical skill, with a focus on understanding diverse perspectives and experiences.

Inclusive Policy Making: Develop policies that actively promote inclusion and diversity in every sphere of society, from workplaces to public spaces. Ensure these policies address not just visible forms of diversity but also invisible challenges, such as mental health and neurodiversity.

Community Dialogues: Foster open dialogues within communities that bridge divides between different races, religions, and social classes. Use these forums not only to discuss challenges but also to celebrate communal achievements and shared goals.

Accessibility and Accommodation: Make accessibility a priority, ensuring that individuals of all abilities have equal opportunities to participate in society. This includes physical accessibility in public spaces as well as accommodations in education, employment, and healthcare.

Interfaith and Secular Cooperation: Encourage cooperation and understanding between religious groups and secular individuals. Highlight common values and goals, and work together on community projects that benefit all members of society.

Support Networks: Create and strengthen support networks that offer assistance and solidarity to those facing health challenges, discrimination, or social isolation. These networks should be adaptable, catering to the specific needs of their members.

Anti-Discrimination Education: Implement comprehensive education programs that tackle biases, classism, and discrimination. Equip individuals with the knowledge and tools to recognize and counteract these behaviors in themselves and others.

A Call to Collective Action

Building a harmonious society is not the responsibility of a select few but a collective endeavor that requires the participation and commitment of all. It's about moving beyond tolerance to active appreciation and support for diversity. It's about creating an environment where empathy and unity are the bedrock of our interactions.

Volunteer and Participate: Engage in community service and volunteer opportunities that allow you to interact with and support individuals from different backgrounds. Such experiences can foster understanding and dismantle stereotypes.

Educate Yourself and Others: Commit to ongoing education about the challenges and experiences of different community members. Share this knowledge within your circles, promoting awareness and understanding.

ADVOCATE FOR INCLUSION: Use your voice and platform to advocate for policies and practices that promote diversity and inclusion. Support leaders and organizations that prioritize these values.

A Symphony of Voices

As we strive to build a harmonious society, let us remember that it is the multitude of voices, each with its own story and struggle, that creates the rich tapestry of our community. By offering our understanding, support, and respect to everyone, we weave together a society that is not only diverse and inclusive but profoundly strong and united. This is not just a vision but a path forward, demanding our attention, action, and unwavering commitment to one another.

Personal Contribution to the Symphony

To contribute to the symphony of voices in building a harmonious society, it's essential to first conduct a self-assessment to identify how you can best serve this vision. Think of society as an orchestra, and yourself as a unique instrument within it. This self-assessment is designed to help you discover your instrument—your unique skills, strengths, and passions—and how you can use it to play your part in this collective endeavor.

Step 1: Identifying Your Instrument

Reflect on Your Strengths: What are you good at? Consider both your hard skills, like writing or technical abilities, and soft skills, such as empathy, communication, or leadership.

Passions and Interests: What are you passionate about? Understanding what drives you can help identify where you might make the most impact.

Learning Style: Are you a visual learner, or do you prefer hands-on activities? Knowing how you learn can guide you toward the roles you'll excel in and enjoy.

Step 2: Tuning Your Instrument

Education and Training: Based on your identified strengths and passions, what additional knowledge or skills do you need to acquire? Consider both formal education and informal learning opportunities.

Practice: Like any instrument, your skills need regular practice. Find opportunities to apply your strengths in real-world settings, whether through volunteer work, projects, or community involvement.

Feedback: Seek feedback from others on your performance and areas for improvement. Constructive criticism is invaluable for growth.

Step 3: Playing in Harmony

Find Your Ensemble: Look for groups, organizations, or movements aligned with your passions. Where does your instrument fit in the orchestra of society?

Collaboration: Learn to collaborate with others whose skills and strengths complement your own. Effective teamwork can increase your impact.

Adaptation: Be open to changing your role or learning new skills as the needs of your community evolve. A versatile musician can contribute to more pieces.

Step 4: Contributing to the Symphony

Community Engagement: Actively participate in community efforts that strive for inclusivity and understanding. Your involvement could range from advocacy and education to supporting those in need.

Lead by Example: Use your actions and voice to inspire others. Share your journey of self-discovery and involvement, highlighting the importance of everyone's contribution.

Continuous Improvement: The needs of society change, and so should your approach. Stay informed, be flexible, and continually seek ways to enhance your contribution to the symphony.

Your Role in the Symphony

This self-assessment is a starting point for understanding how you can contribute to building a harmonious society. Remember, the symphony requires a diverse array of instruments, each playing its part. By identifying your unique instrument and learning how to play it well, you not only fulfill your potential but also enrich the collective melody, creating a society that celebrates diversity, fosters empathy, and promotes unity.

Chapter 8: The Role of Faith and Belief - Embracing Diversity

———

In exploring the role of faith and belief, it's crucial to underscore that this chapter *does not aim to convert or change anyone's religious beliefs*. Instead, it's an invitation to acknowledge and appreciate the profound impact that faith, spirituality, and personal convictions have on individuals' lives and on society. This exploration is about recognizing the diversity of beliefs as a source of strength and enrichment, fostering an environment of mutual respect, and understanding.

Celebrating Diversity in Faith and Belief

Acknowledging Varied Paths: Recognize that the journey toward finding meaning, purpose, and community can take many forms. Each faith, spirituality, or personal belief system offers unique insights, practices, and perspectives that contribute to the rich tapestry of human experience.

Unity in Diversity: Emphasize the commonalities that exist across different belief systems, such as the values of compassion, empathy, and the pursuit of justice. Celebrating these shared values can bring individuals and communities closer, transcending differences.

———

THE IMPACT OF FAITH and Belief Without Conversion

Personal Empowerment: Discuss how faith and belief, in their myriad expressions, empower individuals to lead lives of purpose and integrity. Highlight the role of personal convictions in inspiring acts of kindness, resilience in the face of adversity, and the pursuit of personal and communal well-being.

Social Cohesion: Explore how faith and belief can act as catalysts for social cohesion and understanding. Through community service, interfaith dialogues, and collaborative projects, diverse belief systems can unite people in working towards common goals and addressing societal challenges.

Strategies for Inclusive Engagement

Respectful Dialogue: Encourage open, respectful conversations about faith and belief that seek to understand rather than persuade. These dialogues can be opportunities for learning, growth, and connection.

Inclusive Spaces: Advocate for creating spaces—be it in communities, workplaces, or educational settings—that are inclusive and respectful of all belief systems. Such environments encourage everyone to share and celebrate their traditions and values without fear of judgment or conversion.

Educational Initiatives: Support initiatives that educate about the diversity of world religions and belief systems, highlighting their history, practices, and contributions to society. Knowledge fosters respect and diminishes misconceptions.

A Tapestry of Beliefs

This chapter stands as a celebration of the diverse landscape of faith and belief that enriches our world. It's a recognition that faith and spirituality, in their many forms, are vital components of human identity and society. By embracing this diversity and fostering an environment of mutual respect and understanding, we can build a more compassionate, inclusive world where every individual feels valued and empowered to contribute to the common good. This journey is not about changing beliefs but about enriching our collective human experience through the appreciation and understanding of the myriad paths that people walk.

Self-Assessment for Inclusive Engagement

Creating an inclusive environment and engaging in open dialogue with diverse faith or communities, especially when their beliefs do not align with your core values, requires self-assessment, empathy, and effective communication. Here's a self-assessment guide to help you navigate these interactions while maintaining respect and understanding:

1. Self-Reflection:

Values Examination: Reflect on your own core values and beliefs. Understand what is non-negotiable for you and what aspects of your values can be flexible or open to discussion.

Bias Awareness: Be aware of any biases or preconceptions you might hold about individuals or communities with different beliefs. Recognize that biases can influence your perceptions and interactions.

2. Empathy:

Put Yourself in Their Shoes: Practice empathy by trying to understand the world from the perspective of individuals or communities with different beliefs. What experiences, history, or cultural contexts have shaped their worldview?

Seek Common Ground: Identify common values or shared goals that can serve as a starting point for constructive dialogue. Focus on areas of agreement to build rapport.

3. Open Dialogue:

Active Listening: Develop active listening skills to genuinely hear and understand the perspectives of others. Avoid interrupting or formulating responses while they are speaking.

Non-Judgmental Approach: Maintain a non-judgmental attitude during discussions. Remember that your goal is to understand, not to convince or convert.

4. Effective Communication:

Respectful Language: Choose words that are respectful and inclusive. Avoid derogatory or judgmental language that might escalate tensions.

Ask Open-Ended Questions: Encourage dialogue by asking open-ended questions that invite thoughtful responses. This fosters deeper conversations.

5. Boundaries:

Know Your Boundaries: Determine your boundaries and limits in discussions. Be clear about what topics or behaviors you are not comfortable with and communicate these respectfully.

Respect Others' Boundaries: Respect the boundaries of others as well. If someone expresses discomfort or asks not to discuss a particular topic, honor their request.

6. Conflict Resolution:

Conflict Management Skills: Familiarize yourself with conflict resolution techniques. These skills can help de-escalate tense situations and find common ground.

Third-Party Mediation: In cases of significant disagreements or misunderstandings, consider involving a neutral third party to mediate the discussion and facilitate understanding.

7. Ongoing Learning:

Educate Yourself: Continuously educate yourself about different belief systems, cultures, and faiths. Seek out diverse perspectives through books, documentaries, and engaging with people from various backgrounds.

Cultural Competency: Develop cultural competency to navigate interactions with individuals from diverse backgrounds effectively.

Engaging with individuals or communities whose beliefs differ from your own requires a combination of self-awareness, empathy, effective communication, and respect for boundaries. By self-assessing and actively working on these skills, you can create an inclusive environment where open dialogue is possible, even in the presence of differing beliefs or values. Remember that the goal is not to change others but to foster mutual understanding and respect.

Chapter 9: Case Studies and Real-Life Stories - Navigating Life's Battles

———

In the mosaic of human experience, the most profound insights often emerge from the stories of individuals who have successfully navigated life's battles. This chapter delves into longer narratives, offering intimate portraits of people from diverse backgrounds, cultures, and belief systems. Their journeys serve as powerful case studies, showcasing the triumph of the human spirit and the lessons they have learned along the way. These stories illuminate the path toward personal greatness, resilience, and the pursuit of a meaningful life.

Case Study 1: Embracing Diversity

Narrative: Meet Sarah, a young woman born into a family deeply rooted in their cultural traditions and faith. However, Sarah's journey led her to explore diverse perspectives and beliefs beyond her upbringing. She shares her experiences of forging connections with people from various backgrounds and how this journey enriched her understanding of the world. Sarah's story teaches us the value of open-mindedness and the beauty of celebrating differences.

Lessons Learned: Sarah's narrative illustrates the importance of curiosity, empathy, and the willingness to engage with diverse viewpoints. It reminds us that our own beliefs can coexist harmoniously with an appreciation for the beliefs of others.

Case Study 2: Overcoming Personal Challenges

Narrative: In this story, we follow Mark, a man who faced significant personal challenges, including a debilitating health condition and financial setbacks. Mark's journey to regain his physical and emotional well-being serves as an inspiration. He shares the strategies he employed to overcome adversity, the support networks that sustained him, and the transformative power of resilience.

Lessons Learned: Mark's narrative underscores the resilience of the human spirit and the capacity for personal growth in the face of adversity. His story serves as a testament to the importance of perseverance, self-compassion, and seeking help when needed.

Case Study 3: Building Inclusive Communities

Narrative: This case study introduces us to a community leader named Aisha, who dedicated her life to fostering inclusivity in her diverse neighborhood. Aisha's journey involves initiating dialogues, organizing cultural exchanges, and promoting understanding among residents from various backgrounds. Her story offers valuable insights into the tangible steps we can take to build harmonious, inclusive communities.

Lessons Learned: Aisha's narrative emphasizes the role of individuals in creating environments where diversity is celebrated and respected. Her story highlights the power of small actions in shaping the inclusivity of our communities and fostering unity among neighbors.

Case Study 4: Finding Purpose and Meaning

Narrative: Meet David, a man who embarked on a journey of self-discovery and spiritual exploration. Through his experiences, including meditation, volunteering, and engaging with different faith communities, David found a deep sense of purpose and meaning. His story serves as an inspiration for those seeking to connect with their inner selves and contribute to the well-being of others.

Lessons Learned: David's narrative emphasizes the significance of inner exploration and the quest for personal meaning. It encourages individuals to explore various avenues, from spirituality to service, in their pursuit of a fulfilling life.

A Tapestry of Resilience and Growth

These case studies and real-life stories weave a tapestry of resilience, growth, and human connection. They remind us that while battles may be unique, the capacity to overcome challenges, seek meaning, and build inclusive communities is a shared human experience. The lessons learned from these narratives serve as beacons of hope and guidance for individuals on their own journeys toward personal greatness and a life infused with purpose and empathy.

Your Fight, Your Journey

As we draw the final curtain on this exploration of battles, beliefs, and the pursuit of a meaningful life, it's time to distill the essence of our journey and to issue a call to action for each reader. Throughout this book, we have traversed the landscapes of diverse perspectives, beliefs, and personal stories, finding common threads that bind us as fellow travelers in the human experience. Now, let's summarize the key themes and inspire you to embark on your personal journey, armed with the insights and strategies we've uncovered.

Key Themes Explored:

1. Battles Beyond the Physical: We began by acknowledging that our battles extend beyond the physical realm. We face challenges in the form of societal biases, cultural perspectives, and personal opinions. The journey of exploration beckons us to seek what resonates with our authentic selves, free from external influence.

2. Identifying the Enemies: In Chapter 2, we delved into the adversaries we encounter—principalities, powers, rulers of darkness, and spiritual wickedness. We discovered how these concepts parallel modern challenges, such as systemic injustices, misinformation, and internal struggles.

3. Foundations Worth Fighting For: Chapter 3 explored virtues like personal greatness, honesty, truth, and freedom from envy and jealousy. We learned how these foundations empower individuals and societies to flourish.

4. Tools for the Fight: In Chapter 4, we discussed strategies for positive change, learning from mistakes, persistence, patience, true love, and goodwill. These tools equip us to navigate life's battles with resilience and grace.

5. Misguided Battles: Chapter 5 critiqued societal obsessions with status, celebrity culture, and unachievable dreams. We examined the pitfalls of relying too heavily on opinions, therapy without action, and hollow hypotheses.

6. The Personal Journey: Chapter 6 emphasized the individual's quest for peace and joy, free from external pressures and opinions. We explored the path to self-discovery and fulfillment.

7. Building a Harmonious Society: In the final chapter, we envisioned a diverse and inclusive society that respects individual battles and offers communal support. We outlined strategies for fostering empathy, unity, and understanding among diverse communities.

YOUR FIGHT, YOUR JOURNEY:

Now, dear reader, it's time to reflect on your own journey. What are you truly fighting for? What battles are worth your time and energy? The call to action is an invitation to embark on a personal odyssey—a quest to uncover your authentic self, define your values, and contribute to a harmonious society.

Identify Your Battles: Take a moment to identify the battles that resonate with your core values and beliefs. What causes, virtues, or principles are worth fighting for in your life?

Equip Yourself: Arm yourself with the tools and strategies discussed in this book. Embrace personal growth, resilience, and a commitment to positive change.

Build Inclusivity: Champion inclusivity in your community. Foster understanding and empathy among diverse groups, respecting the beliefs and perspectives of others.

Lead by Example: Be a beacon of hope and inspiration for those around you. Your journey can serve as a model for others seeking meaning and purpose.

Never Stop Exploring: The journey is ongoing. Continuously explore, learn, and grow. Engage with diverse perspectives, cultures, and beliefs to enrich your own path.

A Life Well-Lived

In concluding this book, we invite you to view life as a canvas waiting for your unique brushstrokes. Your fight, your journey—these are the colors that will define the masterpiece of your existence. As you navigate your battles, remember the lessons shared within these pages. Embrace personal greatness, foster understanding, and contribute to the harmonious society we envision.

With resilience, empathy, and a commitment to positive change, you have the power to shape a life well-lived. The battles you choose to fight, guided by your core values and beliefs, will be the brushstrokes that create your own beautiful tapestry of existence. May your journey be meaningful, your heart be open, and your impact be profound. Your fight is uniquely yours, and it's worth every step of the journey.

Appendices

Resources for Further Reading and Exploration

Books on Personal Growth:

"The Power of Now" by Eckhart Tolle

"Daring Greatly" by Brené Brown

"Man's Search for Meaning" by Viktor E. Frankl

Exploring Belief Systems:

"The World's Religions" by Huston Smith

"The God Delusion" by Richard Dawkins

"The Tao of Pooh" by Benjamin Hoff

Diversity and Inclusion:

"Blindspot: Hidden Biases of Good People" by Mahzarin R. Banaji and Anthony G. Greenwald

"White Fragility" by Robin DiAngelo

"Why Are All the Black Kids Sitting Together in the Cafeteria?" by Beverly Daniel Tatum

Personal Development Exercises:

Journaling Prompts for Self-Reflection

Meditation and Mindfulness Practices

Strengths-Based   Assessment   Tools   (e.g.,   Gallup
StrengthsFinder)

Community Building and Empathy:

"The Empathy Effect" by Helen Riess, MD

"Nonviolent Communication" by Marshall B. Rosenberg

Practical Exercises and Reflections

Values Clarification Exercise: Reflect on your core values and beliefs. Write down the values that are most important to you and consider how they align with your actions and choices.

Mindfulness Meditation: Practice mindfulness meditation to cultivate self-awareness and the ability to remain present in the moment.

Empathy Building: Engage in conversations with individuals from diverse backgrounds, actively listening to their perspectives without judgment.

Community Engagement: Get involved in a local community or volunteer organization to experience the power of collective action and building inclusive communities.

Journaling for Growth: Start a journal to record your personal journey, insights gained, and goals for personal development.

Strengths Assessment: Use strengths assessment tools to identify your unique strengths and explore how to leverage them for personal growth and contribution to society.

These practical exercises and reflections are designed to help you apply the insights from the book to your life. They provide a hands-on approach to personal growth, empathy-building, and community engagement, allowing you to embark on your own journey of self-discovery and positive change.

Afterword: Embracing The Tapestry of Life

Dear Friend/Reader,

As I reflect on the journey we've taken together, I am filled with gratitude for the opportunity to share insights from multiple perspectives—those of a minister, a holistic wellness coach, an author, and a human behaviorist. These varied roles have provided me with a unique vantage point from which to explore the tapestry of human experience and the principles of inclusivity, personal growth, and empathy.

From the pulpit, I have witnessed the power of faith and belief in guiding individuals toward lives of purpose and meaning. I have seen the beauty of diverse spiritual traditions and the shared values that unite us as people seeking connection, compassion, and understanding.

As a holistic wellness coach, I have walked alongside individuals on their journeys toward physical, emotional, and spiritual well-being. I have learned that true wellness encompasses not just the absence of illness but the presence of vitality, resilience, and inner peace. It is a path of self-discovery and self-care, a journey that requires us to listen to our bodies, minds, and hearts with compassion.

As an author, I have had the privilege of weaving narratives and ideas into the pages of this book. I have witnessed how stories have the power to inspire, provoke thought, and ignite change. Through these stories, I hope to have conveyed the importance of open dialogue, the value of diverse perspectives, and the beauty of personal growth.

And as a human behaviorist, I have delved into the intricate workings of the human mind and heart. I have marveled at the complexity of our thoughts, emotions, and behaviors, and I have come to appreciate the limitless potential for growth and transformation that resides within each of us.

THROUGH THESE DIVERSE experiences, I have come to a profound realization: that no matter how people theorize, hypothesize, or research, no one can ever create your experience because it is uniquely yours. Your journey, your battles, your beliefs—they are the fabric of your existence, and only you can truly experience them.

So, as we part ways at the end of this book, I offer this simple yet profound truth: Enjoy your experiences. Embrace the diversity of beliefs, perspectives, and battles that make up the tapestry of your life. Let your journey be a source of growth, empathy, and connection. And remember that in the grand symphony of existence, your unique notes contribute to the harmonious whole.

May your life be a testament to the beauty of inclusivity, the power of personal growth, and the richness of human connection. Embrace your journey, for it is a masterpiece in the making.

With heartfelt wishes for your well-being and fulfillment,

Jeremy B Sims

Don't miss out!

Visit the website below and you can sign up to receive emails whenever Jeremy B. Sims publishes a new book. There's no charge and no obligation.

https://books2read.com/r/B-A-CRSAB-PCIVC

BOOKS 2 READ

Connecting independent readers to independent writers.

Did you love *What are YOU fighting for?*? Then you should read *50 Shades of Salvation*[1] by Jeremy B. Sims!

[2]

"50 Shades of Salvation" is an enlightening journey through the diverse landscapes of spiritual practices and personal growth. Authored by Jeremy B. Sims, a seasoned minister, holistic wellness coach, human behaviorist, and motivational speaker, this book invites readers on a profound exploration of the quest for personal salvation. Across its pages, Sims delves into the heart of what it means to seek spiritual fulfillment, blending insights from various religions, cultures, and personal experiences. Each chapter unfolds a new dimension of the journey, from

---

1. https://books2read.com/u/3k91pO

2. https://books2read.com/u/3k91pO

overcoming obstacles and embracing holistic wellness to finding deep connections in relationships and the environment. With a blend of real-life stories, reflective exercises, and practical advice, Sims crafts a guide that encourages continuous exploration, growth, and the pursuit of a harmonious coexistence with the world. "50 Shades of Salvation" is more than a book; it's a companion for anyone seeking to deepen their spiritual journey and live a life of greater purpose, peace, and connection.

Read more at https://www.jbsims.com/.

Also by Jeremy B. Sims

Book 2
From Country Roads to City Penthouses Part 2

Standalone
Awakened Wellness: Are YOU Spiritually Motivated Yet?
Stop Blaming the Adversary: It's You!
From Milk to Meat: The Journey of Spiritual Maturity
Reviving Your Sacred Space: The Call for True Worshippers
Cultivating Self-Discipline: A Path to Personal and Universal
Success
The Morning After
In the Shadow of Holiness
Un Rêve à Washington D.C.
Keep That Temple Clean: A Biblical Perspective
Harboring Harmony: Navigating Through Love, Freedom, and
Moral Rediscovery
and This is just the Beginning
50 Shades of Salvation
What are YOU fighting for?

GOT HUMILITY?

Watch for more at https://www.jbsims.com/.

Printed in the USA
CPSIA information can be obtained
at www.ICGtesting.com
JSHW022101180924
69978JS00002B/72

9 798224 127627